SHORTCUT REAL FOOD

20-minute meals

Christie Kelemen

Bon Appétit

Once upon a time, I spent hours in the kitchen and garden making bread with my own sourdough starter, dehydrating produce from my garden and feeding my family the perfect meals I deeply desired to gift to them. It was bliss!

Now I am a single mother of three with a busy, new career, plus running a business and maintaining a home and yard by myself. I am busy… as most of us are. It took me years to craft a new way of feeding my family where I gave them the nutrition we needed but quickly and in a doable fashion. Now we eat much, much healthier than the average American and I am not exhausted at the end of the day.

This is not your ordinary cookbook. It's not a dry collection of recipes.

Each breakfast, lunch and dinner entry is a full meal, sides included! Also, everything can be made in 20 minutes or less!

The directions include the most efficient order to cook the entire meal in.

All recipes are gluten and lactose free, or list substitutions to make them so, and low/lower sugar.

The goal of this cookbook is to feed oneself and one's family with real, whole, traditional foods (pasture-raised/organic animal foods, organic/local produce and healthy fats - olive oil, avocado oil, coconut oil, pasture-raised butter, nuts and seeds) as quickly and efficiently as possible. (Visit westonaprice.org and nourishingourchildren.org for more information on Real Food.)

It wasn't easy for me to figure out how to do this. I have bought so many cookbooks I never cook from. Either, they are too time consuming, even if they look great, or the recipes are too odd that I, and especially my kids, don't want to eat them. Many real food cookbooks did not even have the amount of time it takes to cook a recipe listed - as if that was irrelevant and only perfection was the standard.

****

If you desire to be healthier, start where you are and make small, incremental changes. This way, the change is not overwhelming and you are more likely to stick with it. Being healthy is not a sprint, it is more of a marathon and you have to pace yourself.

Focus on improving the quality of your food first. Upgrade one food item or group at a time. It is important to buy produce and grains organically, but much more important to purchase organic, grass-fed, pasture-raised, wild-caught animal products. Chemicals accumulate in animals as they eat chemically laden plants, giving you multiple exposures to chemicals. If I have to buy something non-organic it will be produce or grains.

These days modern grocery stores are full of packaged foods that are great for you. Did you actually read that? "Don't eat processed foods! Shop only the edges of the grocery store", is the mantra of many health professionals. It is true, sort of. Most processed foods are the bane of achieving health and well-being. However, that refrigerated bag of organic, chopped kale or the frozen, organic mixed vegetables are amazing for you. There are more and more items available where the work that a home cook would do has been done for you.

When I shop, I focus on buying animal products in their whole, unprocessed forms. Then I look for gems of packaged/prepped foods, in BPA free packaging, that are the produce and grains I can add in. It's a mind shift that some packaged foods are good, but it will free you in the kitchen and allow you to feed your family wonderfully!

I feel free to be back in the kitchen and have it be full of joy again. I couldn't afford to go out to eat for every meal nor did I want to feed my kids junk all the time. **So, I reinvented real food cooking to make it fast and achievable for us regular folks.**

As my youngest says,

"Poof! Magic! Nutrition!"

contents

→

Tip 1:
Cook once, Eat twice (or more).

Make friends with leftovers. Cook extra of your
favorite meal and take it to work
the next day, or the whole week.

QUICK
BREAKFASTS

7

Quick Breakfast Drinks

Visit the "Simple Beverages" section of this cookbook to see the recipes for:

It's a Meal Smoothie (page 111):

Quick Breakfast Drinks

Vanilla Protein Latte (page 103):

Omegaful Bagel Breakfast

serves 4, prep/cooking time 10 minutes

A full breakfast on a bagel!

Ingredients

4 Organic, Sprouted, Whole-grain or
Gluten- Free Bagels

8 oz Pasture-raised Cream Cheese

or Lactose Free Cream Cheese

2 T Fresh Dill

⅛ t Onion Powder

1 Organic Cucumber

4 oz lox (smoked salmon)

Directions

Toast bagels.

Spread cream cheese on both halves
of the bagels. Sprinkle with dill and
onion powder.

Slice cucumber into thin rounds.
Place cucumber slices on top of the
cream cheese.

Place 1 oz of salmon on each bagel.

Fast Oatmeal Packages

serves 5, prep/cooking time 5 minutes

I make five of these on Sunday afternoons for simple, fast breakfasts during the workweek.

Ingredients

5 snack baggies

1 ¼ c Organic Rolled Oats (¼ c per package)

1 ¼ t Cinnamon (¼ per package)

⅝ t Sea Salt (⅛ t per package)

2 ½ T Pasture-raised Butter (½ T per package)

1 c Nuts/Seeds (about 3 T per package)

5 t - 5 T Flax seeds (1 t - 1 T per package)

(2 ½ c water for cooking, ½ c per package)

Directions

Place all ingredients in the five baggies. Store in the refrigerator.

For breakfast, pour a Fast Oatmeal Package in a bowl. Add ½ c water.

Microwave for 1 minute. Stir. Repeat until done to your liking.

Note: Break up the cooking time into 1 minute increments or your oatmeal may boil over. Using a taller bowl will also help this.

Egg in a Basket

serves 1, prep/cooking time 5 minutes

I love both oatmeal and eggs for breakfast! For during the week I looked for a way to have them without cleaning multiple pans. Egg in a basket is the answer!

Ingredients

1 Fast Oatmeal Packet (see Fast Oatmeal Packet recipe)

1/2 c Filtered Water

1 Pasture-raised Egg

pinch of Sea Salt

1/2 c Organic Blueberries

Directions

Pour oatmeal packet in a bowl. Add water and stir. Microwave for 1 minute. Stir.

Crack an egg on top of the oats. Sprinkle with salt.

Microwave for 1 1/2 minutes. Add 30 seconds as needed.

Top with blueberries.

Frambled Eggs Breakfast

serves 4, prep/cooking time 15 minutes

I set out to make meals quicker and have less dishes to clean. So, frambled eggs was invented in my kitchen! Skip the pre-whisking of scrambled eggs and another bowl to clean!

Ingredients

1 T Pasture-raised Butter

6 Pasture-raised Eggs

1lb bag Frozen Mango Chunks

Four slices sourdough or gluten-free bread and pasture-raised butter.

Salt, pepper and additional pasture-raised butter for serving.

Directions

Put mangos in a bowl, cover with water. As you prepare the rest of the meal, drain and refill the bowl with new water until defrosted.

Melt butter in pan over medium heat. Crack eggs into pan. Stir. Stir more as you cook. Salt to taste.

While eggs cook, toast the bread.

PAN-cake Breakfast

serves 4, prep/cooking time 20 minutes

This recipe is so much faster than standing at the stove making stacks of pancakes. And, it has the fresh hint of lemon! Lemon is known for boosting mood and reducing inflammation.

Ingredients

Oven safe, 10" pan

2 T Pasture-raised Butter

5 Pasture-raised Eggs

⅓ c Pasture-raised Milk or Almond Milk

½ Organic Sprouted, Whole Wheat, White or King Arthur's Measure for Measure Gluten Free Flour

2 T Pure Maple Syrup

½ t Sea Salt

3 drops Lemon Vitality Essential Oil (or vanilla extract)

1 package fresh Organic Strawberries

Pure maple syrup and pasture-raised butter for serving.

Directions

Preheat oven to 400 degrees.

Melt butter in oven-safe pan, over medium heat.

While butter is warming, in a large mixing bowl, using a whisk, mix eggs, milk, flour, syrup, salt and lemon. Pour in pan.

Place pan in oven (do this even if the temperature is not yet 400 degrees.) Turn off your stove.

Bake 10-12 minutes until just lightly brown on top.

While the Pan-cake is cooking, rinse and slice strawberries.

Serve with maple syrup and butter.

Ancient Grains Breakfast

serves 2, prep/cooking time 10 minutes

This is a hearty, warm bowl of goodness in the morning!

Ingredients

1 10 oz. package Frozen, Steamed Ancient Grains Mix

¼ t Sea Salt

1 t Cinnamon

¼ c Organic Raisins

1 T Raw Honey

1 T Pasture-raised Butter

¼ c Pecans

Directions

Microwave the grain mix for 3 minutes.

In a medium bowl, mix salt, cinnamon, raisins, honey and butter.

Stir in grains.

Top with pecans.

Crispy Frittata

serves 4, prep/cooking time 20 minutes

We love having hash browns and eggs on the weekend. I wanted a way to use only one pan. The Crispy Frittata was born!

Ingredients

Oven safe, 10" pan

3 T Pasture-raised Butter

8 oz bag Frozen Organic Seasoned Hash Browns

8 Pasture-raised Eggs

½ t Sea Salt

⅓ c Whole Pasture-raised Milk or Almond Milk

½ c shredded Pasture-raised Cheddar Cheese

1 T Chives

14 oz bag Frozen Mangos and Peaches

Directions

Preheat oven to 450 degrees.

Pour fruit into a bowl and cover with warm water.

While the fruit defrosts, heat butter in skillet over high heat. Add hash browns, evenly distributing and pressing down. Cook 3 minutes, then flip one section of the pan at a time. Redistribute hash browns and press down. Reduce heat to medium high. Cook 2 minutes.

While the hash browns are cooking, whisk together eggs, salt and milk.

Once hash browns have cooked the final 2 minutes, pour eggs on top. Sprinkle on cheese. Place in oven, even if not yet to 450 degrees, until eggs are set - about 8 -10 minutes.

While the frittata cooks, drain fruit and refill bowl with warm water. Cut chives with kitchen shears.

Sprinkle frittata with chives and serve with fruit.

Tip 2:
Ask for help in the kitchen.

Make sure to have everyone in your house contribute something to the meal, even if it is just a young child putting forks on the table.

You don't have to do everything yourself!

EASY
SNACKS

Retreat Protein Bars

serves 12, prep/cooking time 20 minutes

I take one to work every day for a low sugar, morning snack! This recipe contains Cinnamon Bark Oil which is known for reducing blood sugar.

Ingredients

¾ c Organic Rolled Oats

1 c Sunflower Seed Butter, stirred so there is not oil at the top, otherwise your bars will be too soft

pinch of Sea Salt

½ t Liquid Stevia

1 T Coconut Oil

2 drops Cinnamon Bark Vitality Essential Oil

1 T Vanilla Extract

½ c Pea Protein Powder

¾ c Organic Raisins

¼ c Mini Chocolate Chips

Directions

Line a 8x8 dish with parchment paper.

Add oats to a food processor. Pulse eight times.

Add the rest of the ingredients, then process until the mixture forms a cohesive ball.

Press into a pan. Fold parchment over the top of the bars to press flat.

Freeze 5 minutes.

Pull out of pan and cut into bars. Store in refrigerator or freezer.

Banana Roll-ups

serves 4, prep/cooking time 10 minutes

These roll-ups are fun! Small children can help make these.

Ingredients

½ c Pasture-raised Ricotta Cheese, or Lactose-free Ricotta Cheese

2 T Sugar

1 t Cinnamon

4 6" Organic Sprouted, Whole Wheat, White, or Gluten-free Tortillas

1 Banana

Directions

In a small bowl mix ricotta, sugar and cinnamon.

Spread ricotta mixture on the tortillas, to the edges.

Slice banana in rounds and place in a row along one edge of each tortilla.

Roll them up.

Easy Biscuits

serves 4, prep/cooking time 20 minutes

A wonderful snack on a cool day with butter, honey and slices of cheese on the side. Leftovers make delicious peanut butter and jelly sandwiches.

Ingredients

½ stick Pasture-raised Butter, cold

2 c Organic Sprouted, White, or King Arthur's Measure for Measure Gluten-free Flour

½ t Sea Salt

1 T Aluminum-free Baking Powder

½ c Pasture-raised Milk, or Almond Milk

Pasture-raised butter, local/raw honey and cheddar cheese slices for serving.

Directions

Heat oven to 450 degrees.

Cut up butter into chunks. Add to a food processor with the flour. Sprinkle on salt. (If you don't have a food processor, try two knives or a pastry cutter, but it will take longer.)

Pulse until butter is chopped into pea sized pieces. Sprinkle on baking powder. Pulse a few more times. Add milk. Mix until a cohesive ball is formed. (Add 1-2 T milk or water if dry.)

Dump onto a floured counter and knead a few times to finish mixing. Pat the dough until you have a 1/2 inch thick round.

Use a small, 2 inch, round cookie cutter to cut the biscuits. (Larger biscuits will take more time to cook.) Repeat. Place biscuits on a baking sheet.

Bake 10-12 minutes until golden brown. While biscuits are cooking, get out what you plan to serve with them.

Beautiful Yogurt Parfait

serves 1, prep/cooking time 5 minutes

Beautiful and delicious!

Ingredients

¾ c Pasture-raised Plain Yogurt, divided, or Lactose-free Yogurt

10 Organic Raspberries

¼ c Organic Blueberries

¼ c low sugar, Organic Granola

1 Organic Strawberry

Directions

In a 12 ounce glass, spoon ⅓ of the yogurt. Add the raspberries, then another layer of ⅓ of the yogurt. Add the blueberries, then another layer of the rest of the yogurt.

Pour on the granola.

Top with the strawberry.

Apple Bowls

serves 4, prep/cooking time 15 minutes

Yummy to-go food! The apple is the bowl - no wasted packaging.

Ingredients

4 Organic Apples

8 T Organic Peanut Butter, 2 T per apple

4 T Organic Dark Chocolate Chips, 1 T per apple

Directions

Use an apple corer, or knife, to remove the core from the apples. Make sure not to cut through the bottom or the filling will fall out.

Fill each apple halfway with peanut butter. Put in some chocolate chips, more peanut butter, and then more chocolate chips.

Spicy Southwest Swirls

serves 6, prep/cooking time 15 minutes

When I was working at one of my first jobs out of college, we often had snack days where we all brought in something to share. I was always asked to bring these!

Ingredients

8 oz Pasture-raised Cream Cheese, or Lactose-free Cream Cheese

½ package Taco Seasoning, or 3 T

1 small Organic Red Pepper (or 2 T diced olives)

4 10" Large Organic, Whole Wheat, Sprouted, or Gluten-free Tortillas

Directions

Place cream cheese in a small bowl. Microwave for 15 seconds. Mix in the taco seasoning thoroughly.

Cut pepper into a small dice.

Spread cream cheese mixture on tortillas (about 4 T per tortilla), covering to the edges.

Sprinkle pepper (or olives) over the tortillas and roll up tightly.

With a serrated knife, cut tortilla wraps into rounds.

No-fuss Grape Popsicles

serves 6, prep time 5 minutes

These simple, no sugar added popsicles disappear out of our freezer before the ones from a box are even open. Get children started cooking with this simple recipe.

Ingredients

Organic Grape Juice

Popsicle holders

Directions

Pour grape juice in holders.

Add tops.

Freeze overnight.

Berry Mint Cottage Cheese

serves 2, prep/cooking time 5 minutes

I eat this snack at the office often in the summer. It carries me through the 3:00 slump when many people are reaching for sugar and caffeine. I make five of them Sunday night to take to work for the week.

Ingredients

½ c Pasture-raised Cottage Cheese, or Lactose-free Cottage Cheese

2 drops Liquid Stevia

½ c Organic Berries of your choice

2 Mint leaves, torn or cut with kitchen scissors

Directions

Place cottage cheese in a bowl. Stir in Stevia.

Add berries and torn mint.

Sweet Apple Sandwiches

serves 4, prep/cooking time 10 minutes

This is a fast, kid friendly snack!

Ingredients

4 Pitted Dates

1 Organic Apple

4 T Pasture-raised Cream Cheese
or Sunflower Seed Butter

Directions

Cut dates in half.

Cut apple in half. Cut out the core. Place the apple cut side down and make 8 slices from each half.

Spread cream cheese or sunflower seed butter on half the apple slices.

Top the spread with a date half and another slice of apple.

Tip 3:
Accept imperfection

You can never be perfect and neither can your food. Follow the 90/10 rule. Eat healthy foods 90% of the time and less healthy food 10% of the time.

Balance is essential in all aspects of eating and living.

FAST
LUNCHES

Salad To-Go Lunch

serves 5, prep/cooking time 10 minutes

When I am not having leftovers for lunch, I pack five of these salads for the week.

Ingredients

5 Storage Containers

10 cups Organic Salad Greens

5 T Cold-pressed, Organic Olive Oil

2 cans of Sweet Potatoes (if they are in a syrup, rinse before using)

5 Snack Baggies

15 T Hemp Seeds, about 1 cup (3 T for each baggy)

2 ½ t Salt (½ t salt for each baggy)

10 T Coconut pieces (not shredded and usually found next to the dried fruit), about 3/4 cup (2 T for each baggy)

10 T Organic Dried Cranberries, about 3/4 cup (2 T for each baggy)

Directions

Place 2 cups salad greens in each of five storage containers.

Add 1 T oil on the side of each container, do not cover the lettuce or it will get a little soggy. Add ⅕th of the sweet potatoes to each container. Cover and refrigerate.

Make the five baggies with the hemp seeds, salt, coconut and cranberries. Store in the refrigerator.

Each work morning, pull out a container, a baggie and a fork.

When you are ready to eat, pour the contents of the baggie onto the salad greens and stir to distribute.

Lunch Protein Stacks To-Go

serves 4, prep/cooking time 15 minutes

These are great to take on the go as everyone heads out for their weekend plans.

Ingredients

1 T Pasture-raised Butter

4 Pasture-raised Eggs

½ t Sea Salt

4 Organic English Muffins, or Gluten-free English Muffins

4 Organic Sausage Patties

4 slices Organic American Cheese

4 Organic Peaches

Directions

Heat butter in skillet over medium heat. Crack eggs in pan.

Flip eggs when one side is done, folding over the sides of the eggs to keep them in compact shapes. Cook until done to your liking. Sprinkle with salt.

While the eggs are cooking, toast the English Muffins until crispy, microwave the sausage patties until hot.

Assemble sandwiches - muffin, egg, sausage, cheese, muffin.

And, each person takes a peach to go.

Lentil Sandwiches Lunch

serves 4, prep/cooking time 15 minutes

This lunch is a throwback from my vegan days. I made this instead of egg salad sandwiches, but I still like it just as much now.

Ingredients

1 can Organic Lentils

4 T Avocado Oil Mayonnaise

¼ t Onion Powder

¼ t Cumin

¼ t Salt

pinch Black Pepper

Eight Slices Sourdough or Gluten Free Bread

Four Organic Lettuce Leaves

4 Baby Cucumbers

4 Baby Bell Peppers

Organic Salad Dressing

Directions

Drain and rinse (and drain well again) the can of lentils.

Mix lentils, mayo, onion, cumin, salt and pepper in a medium bowl.

Get out baby veggies and dressing for dipping.

Spread lentils on bread. Add a lettuce leaf to each sandwich.

Serve with veggies and dip.

Pesto Chicken Salad Lunch

serves 1, prep/cooking time 10 minutes

If you can't find organic, canned chicken locally, Wild Planet's Organic Chicken can be ordered on Amazon. It's key to effortless chicken salad. Small frozen herb cubes are now found in the freezer section of grocery stores.

Ingredients

2 cubes frozen Basil

1 5 oz can Organic Chicken

1 t Garlic Oil

2 t Olive Oil

¼ t Sea Salt

1 T Pasture-raised Parmesan Cheese

1 T Walnuts, broken into pieces

2 Slices of Sourdough or Gluten-free Bread

1-2 Organic Lettuce Leaves

½ Organic Cucumber, sliced

Directions

Take out basil cubes and microwave 15 seconds.

Open and drain the can of chicken. Place chicken, basil, oils, salt, parmesan and walnuts in a bowl. Stir.

Spread chicken mix on bread. Lay lettuce leaves and sliced cucumbers on top.

Grilled Cheese and Apple Lunch

serves 4, prep/cooking time 10 minutes

Finding a good sourdough bread was a game changer for our grilled cheese sandwiches. It added a nice crispness. Also, the sweetness of the apples pairs well with the sourness of the bread.

Ingredients

2 T Pasture-raised Butter

8 Slices Sourdough or Gluten-free Bread

4 Pasture-raised Colby Cheese Slices

1 Organic Red Apple

30 Organic Baby Carrots

Directions

Put 1 T butter in a skillet on medium high heat. Once the butter is melted, lay four slices of bread in the pan. Top with slices of cheese.

Slice apple thinly and put on top of the cheese.

Butter the other slices of bread with the remaining 1 T butter and place them on top.

Cook until each side is golden brown and the cheese is melted.

Serve with carrots.

Salmon, Kale & Cranberry Salad

serves 2, prep/cooking time 10 minutes

This is a superfood lunch that is delicious!

Ingredients

1 bag Cut-up Kale

1 Organic Lemon

2 T Extra Virgin Olive Oil

½ t Sea Salt

⅛ t Black Pepper

½ c from a bag of Grated Organic Carrots

½ c Dried Cranberries

1 6 oz can Wild-caught Alaskan Salmon

Directions

Pour kale into a large bowl. Add in the juice of the lemon & oil and salt & pepper to taste. Using your hands, mix and squeeze the kale to soften it.

Mix in the carrots and cranberries.

Drain the can of salmon and put on top of the kale mixture.

Bean & Cheese Bowl Lunch

serves 4, prep/cooking time 20 minutes

This is an easy dinner that is a crowd pleaser!

Ingredients

1 Package Organic Frozen Rice

1 15 oz can Black Beans

1 ripe Avocado

1 small bag shredded or baby Organic lettuce

8 oz Shredded Pasture-raised Cheddar Cheese

Pre-made Corn Salsa

Pasture-raised Sour Cream

Directions

Cook rice in the microwave according to package directions.

Open and drain the can of beans.

Cut the avocado in half, remove pit and slice.

In four bowls, place the rice, then lettuce, then beans and then cheese.

Top with the avocado slices and dollops of corn-salsa and sour cream.

Cheese & Egg Board Lunch

serves 4, prep/cooking time 15 minutes

A simple lunch to place on the table.

Ingredients

2-4 Pasture-raised eggs

¼ c Olives

1-2 large Organic Apple, sliced thin

2-4 ounces Pasture-raised cheese, sliced

20 Organic Baby Carrots

8 oz Organic Hummus

1 pint Organic Cherry Tomatoes

Directions

Place eggs in boiling water in a saucepan. Cook 10 minutes, drain and cool.

While eggs are cooking, assemble the other ingredients on a cutting board or platter.

Peel eggs, slice and salt. Add to board.

Grilled PB&J Lunch

serves 4, prep/cooking time 15 minutes

When you have nothing on hand and need to fill a bunch of little tummies, this is an easy solution that makes everyone happy.

Ingredients

2 T Pasture-raised Butter

8 Slices Organic Sprouted, White, Whole Grain or Gluten-free Bread

8 T Peanut Butter (or other nut/seed butter)

4 T All-Fruit Jelly

Fruit and Veggie Pouches, or raw vegetables

Directions

Heat large pan over medium heat with 1 T butter.

Spread peanut butter and jelly on half of the bread.

Butter the other slices of bread and place on top of the first set.

Cook until golden brown on both sides.

Serve with fruit and veggie pouches.

Speedy Avocado Lunch

serves 4, prep/cooking time 5 minutes

Nutritious, fast food!

Ingredients

2 Ripe Avocados

pinch of Sea Salt

6 T Organic Salsa

2 Organic Apples

4 Pasture-raised Cheese Slices

Directions

Cut avocados in half. Remove pits. Sprinkle with salt.

Fill avocados with salsa.

Core and slice apples thinly to make "crackers" to put the cheese slices on.

Cut cheese into smaller slices. Sandwich slices of cheese between two apple slices.

Tip 4:
Find a Support System

You can't do it alone.
Some days you'll need back up.

Enlist friends or family when you need help.

Read my blog at **chrsitiekelemen.com**.

STRESS-FREE
DINNERS

"Kids' Love it" Stir-fry Dinner

serves 4, prep/cooking time 20 minutes

Coconut Aminos is my family's go-to sauce. It's a sweet and salty flavor, without soy.

Ingredients

2 T Avocado Oil

1 t Garlic infused Olive Oil

1 lb Pasture-raised Chicken Tenders (breasts will take longer to cook)

1 t Salt

1 bag Frozen, Steamed Organic Rice

1 lb bag Frozen Stir-fry Vegetable Mix

3 T Coconut Aminos, plus additional for serving

Directions

Heat 1T avocado oil and 1t garlic oil in large pan over medium high heat. Place chicken in pan and sprinkle with 1/2 t salt.

Turn chicken when one side starts to brown. Cook until no longer pink. Set aside on a plate on the back of the stove to keep warm.

Microwave rice according to its directions while the rest of the meal cooks.

Heat additional 1 T oil in pan. Cook vegetables until tender.

Add chicken to vegetables. Stir in coconut aminos.

Make Your Own Nachos Dinner

serves 4, prep/cooking time 20 minutes

Everyone gets dinner the way they want it!

Ingredients

8 oz Organic Tortilla Chips, cooked in Avocado Oil or Pasture-raised Lard

8 oz Organic Refried Beans

8 oz Pasture-raised Shredded Colby Jack Cheese

1-2 Organic Tomatoes

Pasture-raised or Lactose-free Sour Cream

Pre-made Guacamole

Pre-made Salsa

2 oz can Sliced, Black Olives

4 Organic Cuties

Directions

Heat oven to 350 degrees.

On a baking sheet, pour out chips. Top with beans and cheese (or half beans and cheese with half just cheese).

Bake 8-10 minutes, until bubbly. (Put in oven even if the temperature is not yet 350 degrees.)

While the chips cook, chop the tomatoes. Put the tomatoes, sour cream, guacamole, salsa and olives in bowls with serving spoons.

Serve with cuties.

Mom's Chicken Noodle Soup Dinner

serves 4, prep/cooking time 20 minutes

I tried all the canned organic, chicken noodle soups I could find. My family only wants this recipe!

Ingredients

1 quart Chicken Bone Broth

6 oz. Organic Spaghetti, or Jovial Brown Rice Pasta

1 lb Pasture-raised Chicken tenders (breasts will take longer to cook)

2 t Organic Olive Oil

1 lb frozen Organic Mixed Vegetables

(carrots, corn, green beans and peas)

Sea Salt (optional)

Directions

Boil broth in a large pot over high heat.

Break pasta in small pieces and cook 5 minutes.

While the pasta cooks, get out the oil, unwrap chicken, get the veggies from the freezer and get out a cutting board and two forks.

Add chicken and oil to the pot and cook 5 minutes, keep water boiling.

Remove chicken and shred with two forks on a cutting board. Return to pot.

Add mixed vegetables, keep water boiling. Cook 3 minutes.

Taste to see if an addition of salt is needed.

Chili & Polenta Dinner

serves 4, prep/cooking time 20 minutes

A great meal for a cold night!

Ingredients

1 lb Pasture-raised Ground Beef

1 T Coconut Oil

1 c Frozen Peppers and Onions

10 oz can Organic Tomato Sauce

15 oz can Organic Crushed Tomatoes

1 t Garlic Oil

1 T Chili Powder

½ t Sea Salt

1 T Oregano

1 can Organic Kidney Beans

2 c Bone Broth

1 tube Organic Polenta

2 t Pasture-raised butter

½ t Sea Salt

1 t Chili Powder

1 c frozen Organic Corn

4 oz shredded Pasture-raised Cheddar Cheese

Directions

Over high heat, add ground beef and oil to a soup pot. While it cooks, add in peppers and onions, tomato sauce, tomatoes, garlic oil, chili powder, salt and oregano. Stir, smash and mix it all up.

Add beans and broth. Boil on high.

Slice polenta in ½" rounds. Place in the bottom of a 8x8 pan, top with pats of butter, chili powder and salt on each slice. Microwave 5 minutes.

Get corn and cheese out.

Remove soup from heat. Add corn.

Top polenta with the chili, or serve on the side.

Serve with cheese.

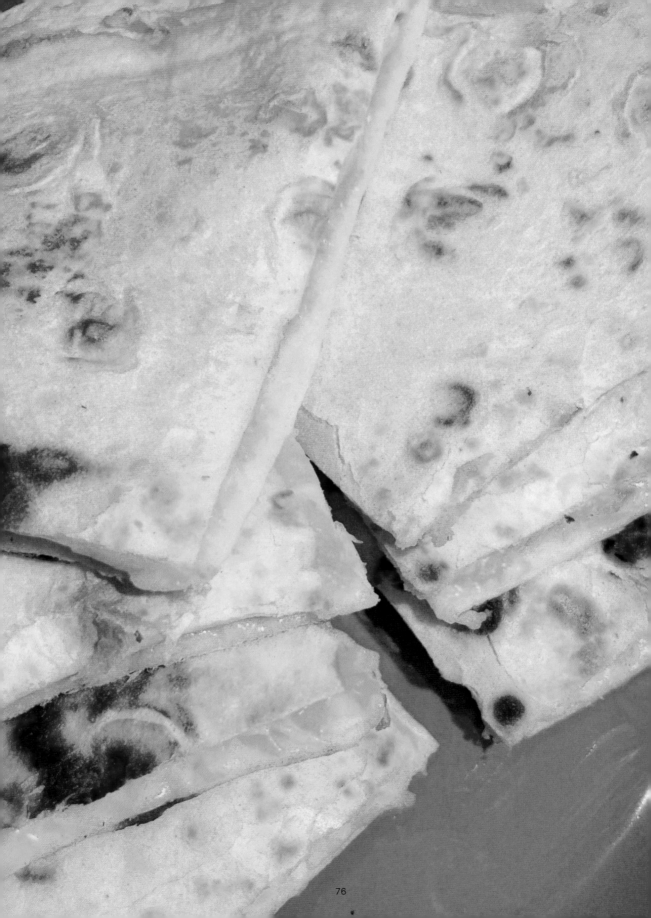

Cheesy Quesadilla Dinner

serves 4, prep/cooking time 20 minutes

This could also be served for lunch. Have leftovers for a snack. I check that the tortillas I buy don't have carrageenan and I get the fat-free beans to avoid added soy, cottonseed or canola oil.

Ingredients

Oil for the pan

1 Package Organic or Gluten-free Tortillas, 8"

1 16 oz can Organic Refried Beans

12 oz Cheddar or Colby Cheese, shredded

6 oz bag Organic Frozen Mixed Vegetables

1 t Pasture-raised Butter

Fresh cilantro

Organic salsa

Pasture-raised Sour Cream

Directions

Wipe your pan with a little oil, heat to medium high.

Spread 1/4 c beans on one tortilla, sprinkle on 2/3 cup cheese and top with another tortilla.

Start cooking the first quesadilla while you make the next one.

Flip when one side is lightly browned. Remove when both sides are done. Repeat.

While those cook, put the vegetables in a pot with ½ c water over medium high. Stir. Cook until tender. Drain. Add butter.

Put the leftover beans in a bowl with cheese sprinkled on top. Microwave for a few seconds. Serve as a side.

Serve with torn cilantro, salsa and sour cream.

"More Please" Spaghetti Diner

serves 4, prep/cooking time 20 minutes

My children ask for this more than once a week!

As always, check the oils in any packaged foods - the pasta sauce should only have olive oil.

Ingredients

Filtered Water for Cooking

½ t Sea Salt

1 lb Organic Pasta, or Jovial Brown Rice Pasta

1 t Coconut Oil

1 t Garlic Oil

1 lb Grass-fed Ground Beef

½ t Salt

1 20 oz jar Organic Pasta Sauce

6 oz Organic Frozen Broccoli

1 t Pasture-raised Butter

2 oz Pasture-raised Parmesan Cheese

Directions

Bring a large pot of water to boil with 1/2 t salt. Add pasta. Cook stirring until tender. Drain.

While the pasta cooks, heat oils in a large pan over medium heat until hot but not smoking, add beef and ½ t salt. Stir, chop and cook until no longer pink. Add pasta sauce until heated.

While meat is cooking add broccoli to a small saucepan with a couple tablespoons of water. Cook until tender. Turn off heat. Drain, if needed. Stir in butter. Serve on the side.

Serve pasta with the Parmesan cheese on the side for each person to add their own.

Hearty Beef Stew Dinner

serves 4, prep/cooking time 20 minutes

Using steak makes this ultra fast. For the same amount of hands on time, you can use stew meat and cook for 2-3 hours (adding the vegetables half way through).

Ingredients

1 T Pasture-raised Butter

1 lb Pasture-raised Steak

½ t Sea Salt

½ t Tumeric

1 t Thyme

¼ t Black Pepper

1 t Garlic Oil

6 T Organic Ketchup (or tomato paste)

2 c Bone Broth

1 c Filtered Water

8 Baby Organic Frozen Potatoes, or Potato Chunks

6 ounces Frozen Organic Carrots

Directions

Heat butter over medium-high heat in a large pot. Cube and add meat. Sprinkle with salt. Cook meat just until lightly brown.

Add turmeric, thyme, pepper, garlic oil and ketchup. Stir. Add broth and water.

Cook 5 minutes.

Defrost frozen ingredients in the microwave, about 4 minutes.

Add the vegetables. Cook 5 minutes.

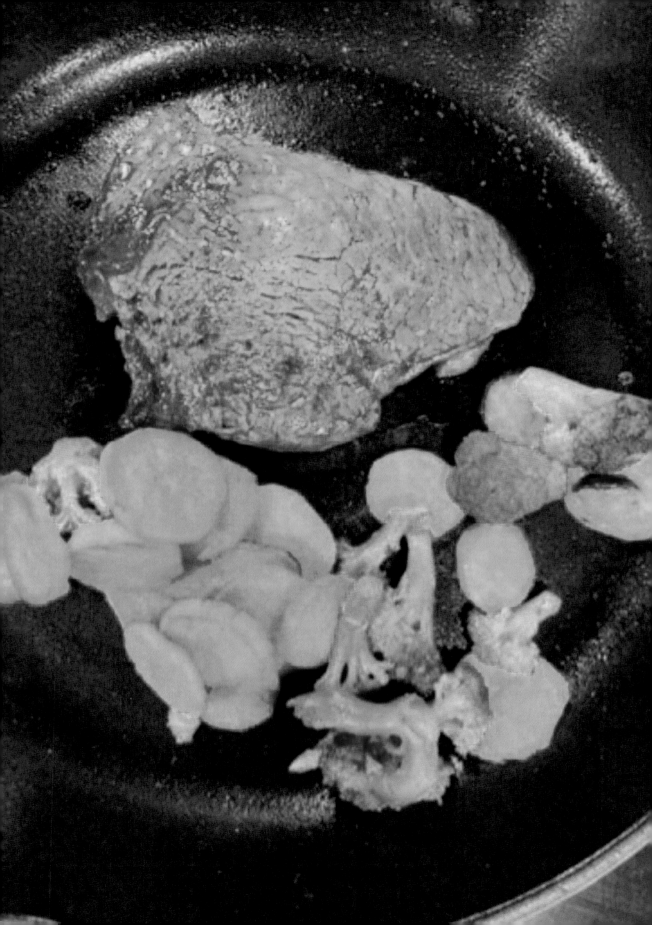

Steak Dinner for One

serves 1, prep/cooking time 20 minutes

A gourmet meal just for one!

Ingredients

2 t Pasture-raised Butter

½ c sliced or cubed Organic Sweet Potato

6 frozen Organic Broccoli Florets

2 pinches Sea Salt

3 oz Pasture-raised Steak

Directions

Heat 1 t butter in skillet over medium high heat.

Cook sweet potato in butter for 4 minutes. Add broccoli. Cook 4 more minutes. Sprinkle with salt. Remove from pan. Add 1 t butter.

Sear steak on both sides. Turn down to medium heat. Cook steak for 4 minutes on each side, depending on thickness. Sprinkle with salt to taste.

Return vegetables to pan to warm up.

"I Vote for Tacos" Dinner

serves 4, prep/cooking time 20 minutes

My youngest was given a t-shirt that says, "I vote for tacos." Every time I see it, I want to make tacos for dinner!

Ingredients

1 t Coconut Oil

1 lb Pasture-raised Ground Beef

2 T Taco Seasoning

1 Organic Tomato

2-4 T Organic Cilantro

1 small bag shredded or baby Organic Lettuce

8 Taco Shells

4 oz Shredded Pasture-raised Cheddar Cheese

Taco Sauce

1 small bag of Organic Baby Carrots to serve on the side

Directions

Heat oil in a skillet over medium high heat. Cook ground beef and taco seasoning until beef is no longer pink.

While the meat cooks, chop the tomato and cilantro.

Get out the rest of the ingredients.

Lay everything out as a buffet for everyone to assemble their own.

Tuna Noodle Dinner

serves 4, prep/cooking time 20 minutes

This dish is warm and creamy and even kids who don't love fish will eat it!

Ingredients

4 Quarts Filtered Water

1 t Sea Salt

12 oz Organic or Jovial Brown Rice Spaghetti

1 c Frozen Organic Peas

2 t Pasture-raised Butter

2 t Onion Powder

⅛ t Garlic Powder

1 c Pasture-raised or Lactose-free Milk

½ t Organic Corn Starch

6 oz can of Wild-caught Tuna

½ c Shredded Pasture-raised Cheddar Cheese

1 T Pasture-raised Parmesan Cheese

Directions

Fill a medium pot with water, adding ½ t salt. Cover while heating.

Cook noodles in high boiling water until al dente.

While the noodles are cooking, measure out peas and let sit to defrost.

In a large pot, melt butter, onion powder and garlic powder over medium heat. Whisk in milk, cornstarch and ½ t salt, cooking and stirring 5 minutes, until thick and bubbly.

Drain pasta and add to sauce along with tuna.

Stir in cheddar cheese.

Sprinkle parmesan on top.

Texas Casserole Dinner

serves 4, prep/cooking time 20 minutes

Yee Haw! A fast and easy dinner in one pan!

Ingredients

Large Oven-Proof Pan

2 t Coconut Oil

1 lb Pasture-raised Ground Beef

2 T Taco Seasoning

15 oz can Organic Crushed Tomatoes

4 oz can Organic Green Chilis

8 Sprouted or Organic Corn Tortillas

8 oz Pasture-raised Cheddar or Colby Jack Cheese, shredded

1 Organic Green Apple

1 small bag "Salad Base Mix" of Chopped Lettuce, Cabbage, Carrots, etc.

2 T Olive Oil

2 t Apple Cider Vinegar

½ t Sea Salt

⅛ t Black Pepper

Directions

Preheat oven to 450 degrees.

Heat oil in a large oven proof pan over medium-high heat. Cook ground beef with taco seasoning until no longer pink.

While beef is cooking, open the cans and drain if needed. Place tortillas in a stack and cut into 1" pieces.

Add tomatoes, chilis and tortillas to beef. Keep pan on high and heat, stir just to distribute. Top with cheese. (Turn off stove.)

Bake 8-10 minutes until cheese is bubbly.

While the casserole bakes, grate apple with a box grater. Add to salad base mix in a bowl. Toss with oil, vinegar, salt and pepper.

Local Sausage Dinner

serves 4, prep/cooking time 20 minutes

I have only been able to find pasture-raised sausage from local farmers. Make friends with your local farmer and see what goodies you can source from him or her! Here in Texas I use FarmhouseDelivery.com.

Ingredients

1 lb baby Frozen Seasoned Potatoes

1 t Coconut Oil

4 Pasture-raised Sausage Links

½ t Sea Salt

dash of Black Pepper

1 T Pasture-raised Butter

¼ c Pasture-raised Milk, or Almond Milk

Directions

Place potatoes in a saucepan covered with water. Over high heat, bring to a boil. Boil 10 minutes until they break apart easily with a fork. (If your potatoes are large, microwave them for a few minutes before boiling them.)

While the potatoes cook, heat a skillet over medium heat with oil. Add sausages. Cook, turning, until internal temperature reaches 160 degrees.

Get out the rest of the ingredients, a strainer and a masher.

Drain potatoes and return to saucepan. Add salt, pepper, butter and milk. Mash well. Serve on the side with the sausage

Pizza Night Dinner

serves 4, prep/cooking time 20 minutes

I use a very small amount of pepperoni to give the pizza extra kid-appeal and add in antioxidant rich basil to give a boost of heath - and serve with a green salad!

Ingredients

1 Premade Sourdough, White, Whole Wheat or Gluten-free Pizza Crust

2 t Olive Oil

6 Pepperoni slices (freeze the rest)

2-4 T Jarred Pizza Sauce (freeze the rest, or add more sauce as your family likes)

20 Fresh Organic Basil Leaves

8 oz. Pasture-raised, Shredded Mozzarella

3 T Olive Oil

1 T Apple Cider Vinegar

2 t Italian Seasoning

½ t Sea Salt

Small bag of Chopped or Baby Organic Lettuce

1 Organic Cucumber

1 pint Organic Cherry Tomatoes

Directions

Preheat oven to 475 degrees.

Brush crust with oil.

Dice pepperoni.

Top crust with sauce, basil, cheese and then pepperoni. Place in oven, even if the temperature is not yet 475 degrees, for about 10 minutes until bubbly.

Meanwhile, in the bottom of a medium bowl, mix the oil, vinegar, Italian seasoning and salt. Add the lettuce and toss.

Dice the cucumber. Top salad with cucumber and tomatoes.

Cod with Quinoa Dinner

serves 4, prep/cooking time 20 minutes

Mild fish is most accepted by those who have not grown to love fish yet. If you use frozen cod, defrost in the refrigerator overnight. (In a pinch, if you forget to defrost the fish, add about 5 minutes to the cooking time.)

Ingredients

1 c Filtered Water

1 t Sea Salt

2 T Pasture-raised Butter

1 t Lemon Pepper Seasoning

1 lb Wild-caught Alaskan Cod

1 pouch Cooked, Seasoned Quinoa

1 c Organic Peas

Directions

Add 1 c water to a skillet, 1 t salt, 1 T butter and lemon pepper seasoning. Bring to a boil.

Place cod in the skillet, cover and reduce heat to medium low. Cook 10 minutes or until the fish just flakes easily.

Microwave peas 3 minutes. Add 1 T butter and peas to quinoa in a small bowl. Microwave 1 minute and stir.

Asian Lettuce Wraps Dinner

serves 4, prep/cooking time 20 minutes

This is a healthy version of the popular take-out meal!

Ingredients

2 t Olive Oil

1 t Garlic Infused Oil

1 lb Pasture-raised Ground Beef or pork

¼ t Red Pepper Flakes

1 t Dried Ginger

½ t Sea Salt

1 bag Frozen, Steamed Organic Rice

½ c shredded Organic Carrots

1 c Organic Broccoli Florets

2 Organic Green Onions

½ c Basil, Cilantro, Mint, or a combination

¼ c Peanuts

1 lime

2 t Coconut Aminos

1 small head Organic Butter or Boston Lettuce

Directions

In a large pan, heat oils over medium high heat. Add the ground meat, red pepper flakes, ginger and salt. Cook until browned - about 5 minutes.

While the meat cooks, cook rice in microwave according to directions.

Add carrot to the cooking meat. Finely chop the broccoli and add to the meat. Finely chop green onions and herbs and add to the meat.

Stir in peanuts, lime and Coconut Aminos.

Serve with lettuce leaves and rice.

Lay out as a buffet for each person to assemble their own.

Tip 5:
Nourish Yourself

nourish (noun)

the act or process of nourishing or being nourished

-Merriam-Webster's dictionary

Many things nourish us besides just food. Pay attention to where you receive nourishment in other areas of your life and spend more time there!

SIMPLE BEVERAGES

My Chai Latte

serves 1, prep/cooking time 10 minutes

When I order Chai Tea from the coffee shops, it is always too sweet. And, when I want something at the end of the day, I don't want caffeine in it. Therefore, I created My Chai Latte.

Ingredients

4 oz. of Filtered Water

1 Herbal Chai Tea Bag

4 oz. Coconut Milk

1 t Organic Sugar or 2 drops Stevia

Directions

In a large mug, microwave the water for 2 minutes.

Add the tea bag and steep for 7 minutes.

Add the coconut milk and sugar or stevia.

Microwave for 1 minute. Stir.

Vanilla Protein Latte

serves 1, prep 5 minutes

This warm drink provides a big hit of protein with no sugar or dairy. I have it every morning in the fall and winter. It is like a hug in a cup!

Ingredients

8 oz Almond Milk

1-2 T Coconut Milk

1 Scoop Amy Meyer's Paleo Protein Powder - Vanilla

Optional - cinnamon

Directions

In a large mug, microwave the almond and coconut milk for about 1 ½ minutes.

Add protein. Whisk. Let sit 1 minute. Whisk again until smooth.

Sprinkle with cinnamon.

Southern Hibiscus Sun Tea

serves 4, prep/cooking time 15 minutes

I live in southern Texas. We have lots of heat and sun here. A fun way to make tea without heating up the house is to make Sun Tea.

Most southerners drink their tea sweet - I add a hint of juice instead of sugar.
Mason jars are convenient because you can take them to go.

Ingredients

4 Organic Hibiscus Tea Bags

2 quarts Filtered Water

2 Mason Jars

½ c Organic Apple Juice, ¼ c for each jar

Directions

The fast way: Place two tea bags in each jar. Cover with boiling water. Steep 5 minutes.

The fun way: Place two tea bags in each jar. Cover with water. Put on lids. Place outside in the sun on a hot day for two hours.

Remove tea bags and pour in juice.

Refrigerate.

Pink Smoothie

serves 2, prep/cooking time 5 minutes

A quick and easy snack filled with vitamins.

Ingredients

1 ½ c Frozen Organic Strawberries

¼ c Frozen Pineapple

1 c Frozen Mango

½ c Organic Orange Juice

1 c Pasture-raised Whole Milk (or more for easy blending), or Almond Milk

Directions

Add fruit, then liquids, to a high-speed blender.

Blend until very smooth.

Chocolate Milk - Two Ways

serves 1, prep/cooking time 5 minutes

My kids and I used to melt dark chocolate, vanilla and sugar in a pan to make chocolate syrup. Then, I found a syrup at the grocery store that has only those ingredients. It's so simple and quick to use this, and it's the same thing. If you are craving a milkshake, this cold version is a great substitute using raw milk.

Ingredients

8 oz Whole Pasture-raised Milk, or Almond Milk

1 T Chocolate Syrup

For the hot version add:
1 Corn Syrup Free and Dye Free Marshmallow

Directions

Cold: Pour chocolate down the sides of the glass. Add milk. A straw makes it more fun!

Hot: Pour milk and chocolate into a mug and microwave for 1 ½ minutes. Add marshmallow and microwave 20 seconds more.

It's a Meal Smoothie

serves 1, prep/cooking time 5 minutes

When I am eating a meal by myself and need something fast, this smoothie is exactly what I need.

Ingredients

1 c Organic Frozen Fruit (I like strawberries and mangos.)

⅔ c Organic Almond Milk or Pasture-raised Milk

2 scoops Organic Pea Protein Powder

1 T Organic Ground Flax Meal

1 handful of something green (I like Fresh Mint and Kale.)

Directions

Add all ingredients to a high speed blender.

Blend until very smooth.

Tip 6:
Run your dishwasher often.

Frequently running your dishwasher allows you to put your cooking pots, pans and baking dishes in. You likely want to spend as little time as you can handwashing. If the dishwasher fills up, soak pans in warm water while they wait for the next dishwasher cycle.

If hand washing dishes is inevitable, I hope you are inspired by the poem below. My mother cut it out of a newspaper when I was a child and had it sitting on the kitchen window sill:

Thank God for dirty dishes, they have a tale to tell.

While other folks go hungry, we are eating very well.

With home and health and happiness,

we shouldn't want to fuss.

For by this stack of evidence, God is very good to us.

-author unknown

EFFORTLESS
DESSERTS

Berry Fruit Crisp

serves 8, prep/cooking time 20 minutes

With the first chill in the air comes my cravings for this fruit crisp.

Ingredients

1 21 oz, or larger, can of Low Sugar Blueberry Fruit Filling

2 c Low Sugar Granola

½ c Organic Flour, or King Arthur's Measure for Measure Gluten-free Flour

2 t Filtered Water

4 T Pasture-raised Butter, cut into chunks

Directions

Heat oven to 450 degrees.

Pour filling into a 8x8 dish.

In a food processor, pulse granola, flour and water 15 times. (If you do not have a food processor, use two knives or a pastry cutter - though it will take longer.)

Sprinkle butter on top and process until mixture is uniform, about 45 seconds. Sprinkle topping over filling.

Bake 10-12 minutes until top is golden. (Place in oven even if it has not reached 450 degrees yet.)

Chocolate Protein Mousse

serves 6, prep/cooking time 20 minutes

This is the best snack I have ever had. It is delicious and I feel proud of myself for being good to my body.

Ingredients

1 can Coconut Milk

¼ c Water

½ c Cocoa Powder

Pinch of Salt

3 scoops Amy Meyer's Paleo Protein, Vanilla Flavored

Variation:

Peppermint - Chocolate

Add 2 drops Peppermint Vitality Essential Oil

Directions

Blend all ingredients in a bowl with a hand mixer.

Pour into individual containers and chill.

Blender Strawberry Ice Cream

serves 4, prep/cooking time 10 minutes

Smooth, sweet, low sugar, soft-serve strawberry ice cream. Yum!

Ingredients

High-speed Blender

1 can Full-Fat Coconut Milk

16 oz Frozen Organic Strawberries

2 T Maple Syrup

Directions

Pour coconut milk, strawberries and maple syrup into a high speed blender.

Blend until the consistency of thick, smooth ice cream. Serve immediately.

Oatmeal Chocolate Chip Bake

serves 16, prep/cooking time 20 minutes

This recipe is great for a special occasion or when you have a crowd over!

Ingredients

1 stick Pasture-raised Butter

2 c Organic Sprouted, White, Wheat, or King Arthur Measure for Measure Gluten-free Flour

½ c Organic Rolled Oats

½ c Organic Brown Sugar

½ c Organic White Sugar

½ t Aluminum-free Baking Soda

½ t Sea Salt

1 Pasture-raised Egg

¼ c Pasture-raised Milk

1 t Pure Vanilla Extract

½ c Organic Dark Chocolate Chips

Directions

Preheat oven to 475 degrees. Butter a 9"x13" pan.

In a small dish, melt butter in microwave, about 1 minute.

In a large bowl, with a hand mixer, briefly mix flour, oats, brown sugar, white sugar, baking soda and salt in a large bowl.

Add egg, milk, vanilla and butter on top of the dry mixture. Wisk these together on top of the dry mixture before stirring them fully in. Mix all just until combined. Mix in chocolate chips.

Put in pan and flatten with your hands. Bake 10-12 minutes until golden brown. (Put the dish in the oven even if it has not reached 475 degrees yet.)

Scoop and serve warm.

(Warm leftovers.)

Cooked Autumn Fruit

serves 4, prep/cooking time 15 minutes

Warm fall fruit on a cool evening is the best treat!

Ingredients

2 T Pasture-raised Butter

2 Organic Red Apples

2 Organic Pears

(or just apples or just pears)

1 t Cinnamon

Pinch of Sea Salt

2 T Sugar

Directions

Heat butter in a skillet over medium high heat.

Core and slice fruit thin. The thinner the slices are, the faster they will cook.

Place fruit in pan and stir. Add cinnamon, salt and sugar.

Continue to stir occasionally until fruit is soft.

In a Flash Mug Cake

serves 1, prep/cooking time 8 minutes

If you can't resist a sugar craving, instead of eating the entire bag of cookies in your pantry, enjoy a small treat. This dessert is a single serving so there is not an opportunity to overindulge. And, it contains a whole protein to balance the sugar.

Ingredients

1 T Pasture-raised Butter

4 T Organic Flour, or King Arthur Measure for Measure Gluten-free Flour

1-2 T Organic Sugar

1 Pasture-raised Egg

1 T Pasture-raised Milk, or Almond Milk

½ t Pure Vanilla Extract

¼ t Aluminum-free Baking Powder

Directions

Melt butter in microwave, 30 seconds.

Add the flour and sugar to the mug, then the egg, milk and vanilla. Whisk the wet ingredients at the top of the mug together until well mixed.

Sprinkle on the baking powder and stir everything in the mug until it looks like cake batter. Don't over mix.

Microwave 45 seconds. Add 15 seconds of baking time until the cake springs back to the touch and looks slightly dry on top.

Let stand one minute.

Tip 7:
I forgot to defrost that!

It happens to everyone –

you forget to defrost something from the freezer before cooking it. You can use your microwave to defrost on the "defrost" setting, but delicate items don't fare well in the microwave.

If you need to defrost something such as fish or fruit, place the item in a bowl in your sink and run cold water over it. Meat even has a better consistency when done this way.

About ChristieKelemen.com

Life is already complicated.

Wellness does not need to be.

Hi. My name is Christie.

When my children were younger they gave me a small magic wand because we said that mamas wave their wand and make magic happen. Now I make magic in the kitchen and help others make magic in their lives. I am the Magician of Nutrition!

I am a busy mom that knows the value of nutrition and health. But, who has time for that?! In realty, who doesn't? Health is one of the most valuable gifts we have.

**Still, how does one get a healthy meal on the table after a long day of work?

**What if food is your go to for stress relief?

**What about when you no longer feel as vibrant, strong and sexy as you once did?

**How do you sort through all the wellness information out there to find out what is right for you?

I have made it through health and life challenges and so can you with the right tools and support!

I created the company, Christie Kelemen, because I wanted to be the change I want to see in the world. My website, christiekelemen.com, is the home of The Easy Healthy Eating blog with ongoing tips for easy healthy eating, simple nutrition, wellness and the home of my online wellness programs.

index

→